Bruised,
But Not Broken

Bruised,

But Not Broken

Overcoming Molestation and Abuse

Sherena Frazier-Miller

Copyright

The Butterfly Typeface Publishing
PO BOX 56193
Little Rock Arkansas 72215

Dedication

For those who feel unloved ...

My love of butterflies goes back to when I was a child. I recall placing grass in the bottom of a jar and having my mom make holes in the lid. Then I would go outside and catch a butterfly. Because I had no siblings, I considered these beautiful creatures my friends. The love I had for my dolls, stuffed animals, and butterflies gave me hope that better days would come.

"I am a victim, yet
I am victorious"

Table of Contents

Foreword

The life of a butterfly is a complicated one. It starts out encased and confined. Although restricted, it's very essence is to struggle and emerge victorious and beautiful. The abuse I endured as a child is reminiscent of the plight of a butterfly.

I was bound and had to endure struggle in order to reach my true purpose. Like the butterfly, I am convinced that it was my struggle that gave way to my beauty for as we have come to learn, an emergence too soon leads to the destruction of the butterfly.

God knew my purpose before I was born. He knew that in order for me to perform the work I was purposed, I had to experience the pain. He also knew that I would have the strength to not only endure, but to survive so that I may now empower others to do the same.

Acknowledgments

Unfortunately, molestation is a huge secret that is rarely shared by the victims. I have been blessed. God has always been there for me. I know He cares. I have a wonderful husband, Troy. He has been by my side even as a young child helping me.

Troy has always cared about my welfare and what was going on with me inside that house. Thank you, Troy, for the years of support you have shown me.

Auntie Lady Gilmore, thank you for always doing your best to save me from what was going on in my home. Auntie, I thank you for always showing me support when I have my bad days.

I still need to talk about the horrible things that happened to me as a child which is why I chose to write this book. I hope and pray that it will help someone else who is struggling to find peace in their life.

Preface

Life Altering

Abuse of any kind is a life altering, unwanted experience. As an only child, I suffered years of molestation in and outside of my home. The abuse was perpetrated upon me by my mother's live-in boyfriend.

The abuse began when I was about seven-years-old and it continued until I was seventeen or eighteen. Several times during my life, I tried to tell my mother about the abuse. She ignored me and later denied that the abuse occurred at all.

She did not want to appear to be an unfit mother.

Only God knows what my mom was feeling, but I can only share what I felt. In my opinion, my mom was not the mother I deserved. Although she is still alive and I have some feelings for her, I do not have a desire to see her. She never cared about what was going on in my life while I was growing up. Therefore, I felt neglected and unwanted at a very young age. These feelings still come back to haunt me.

I'm not judging her, but while I don't think she cared for me, I do believe my mother genuinely cared for her boyfriend. We lived in a two-family house on East 139 Street off Union in Cleveland, Ohio. The lady that lived downstairs was also our landlord.

Although I do not know for sure, I believe she had an idea of what was going on with me in the upstairs apartment. She always tried to have me stay downstairs with her while my mother was at work. Unfortunately, at some point, I would have to return upstairs to prepare for bed.

After my shower, I would leave the bathroom headed for my bedroom. It seemed *he* always knew when I was heading for my room, because often he would be there to greet me. He had a terrible drug habit which frightened me.

From time to time, during those years, my abuser would go to prison. He never stayed locked up long enough for me to experience any real measure of peace.

To add insult to injury, my mother would force me to visit him in prison whenever she would go. I had no choice because visiting him was part of her rules. He caused so much pain in my life. I never felt like my home was a home because I never felt safe. Consequently, I would run away from home trying to escape how badly I felt about him, what was happening to me and even how I felt about myself. I still suffer from issues of low self-esteem today.

The years of sexual abuse have affected my life in many ways; however, I absolutely refuse to live my life depressed and burdened with my past. Even though I feel I have moved forward, there are many moments when I feel abandoned. I continue to feel isolated by some family members.

Frequently, especially in my teenage years, I spent time with my grandfather. Very few family members seemed to care about my welfare, but my grandfather happened to be one who deeply cared about me.

Parents listen to your children when they tell you that someone is touching them. Take the time to find out the truth about what your child believes. As a parent, you are your child's first line of defense against any harm.

Recently, I received a Criminal Justice Degree. My goal is to use this degree to raise awareness of childhood molestation in hopes of substantially reducing the cases of it occurring.

I am also writing this book in order to share more details of my life with readers. I will no longer allow people to say painful and hurtful things to me. This book is about me standing in my truth and refusing the thoughts and opinions of others to determine my destiny.

Introduction

The Beginning

My name is Sherena; I was born and raised in Cleveland, Ohio in 1971. This book will explain how it was growing up as an only child and living in a home dealing with childhood molestation.

My mother had a live-in boyfriend named Al. I grew up believing that he was my father and that he and my mom were married. When I was around four, we lived in a house on East 115th Street off of Superior in Cleveland, Ohio. My bedroom was upstairs.

One night I was scared because the house was dark, but I was also afraid to ask my mother to turn the lights on. I just kept crying. I heard Al tell her to go and handle me; she came into the room and beat me. She used a Eureka vacuum cleaner cord to beat me. I went to sleep after being whipped. I had been whipped so hard that the next morning I was unable to open one of my eyes.

My mother took me to Metro Hospital in Cleveland, Ohio; I was admitted to the hospital and stayed for several days. I cannot recall if any operations took place, but I know I wore a patch over my eye for many days. I can also remember Pastor J.W. Haynes praying for me. I disliked my mother for beating me that night, and I could not understand why she would beat me so severely. I never felt loved by my mother after that beating.

While I was in the Hospital, a man came to see me. He said he was my father. His name was Robert. He spent some time with me, and he left.

Maybe a year or two later, we moved to Steinway off Buckeye in

Cleveland, Ohio. I started school at Buckeye-Woodland in Cleveland. I was the little girl who had major problems and felt strange most of the time.

One day I locked myself in a locker. I was five-years-old at the time. The school called my mother. She came to the school and wanted to know why I had gotten inside of the locker. I didn't have any answers for her. Perhaps, I wanted a place where I felt safe.

After a few years, we moved to 3557 East 139 Street off Union in Cleveland, Ohio. There was a lady who lived downstairs, named Mrs. Max; she was nice to me. I loved her very much.

I recall the molestation starting once we moved on East 139 Street. One evening I was lying on the sofa. Al sat next to me and started tickling me while my mother was sleeping in the other room.

He began to rub my chest, then he made me rub his penis. I was so confused. I did not know what to do or to think. I was only seven-years-old. After that event had taken place, I tried to stay away from him. It was hard to do because we were living in a two- family house.

(The house was a one-family home that the owner converted into a two-family home.) It wasn't large enough to hide from my abuser.

My bedroom was the size of a closet with just a twin bed and dresser. I knew I was not able to talk to my mother about what had happened. Al told me she would not believe me if I said anything to her. He also said he would whip my butt.

After that first event, Al started to come into my room at night and get in the bed with me while my mother was asleep. For some reason, I felt like my mom was not always sleeping. I used to think she was aware of what was going on.

Al had a son named Alex who was younger than me. Alex would spend the night sometimes. I was glad when he would spend the night because I felt safe. Al would not bother me because his son was in the house. Al would stay away from me when his son was over; I guess he did not want his son to see him acting like the crazy man he was.

Chapter Two

New House More Drama

Between 1984-1985, we moved from East 139 Street to a new address 12321 Signet Cleveland, Ohio which was ten minutes from the old house. I was hurt and sad that we had to move. The lady downstairs (Mrs. Max) at my previous home on East 139 Street was loving and caring. She used to take me shopping and treat me with respect. Her family was kind to me, and I enjoyed being around them. I knew once we moved things would never be the same again.

The house where we moved belonged to the nephew of Mrs. Max. His name was Howard. I was happy that I finally had a real bedroom that was large enough to hold two twin beds, a dresser, a chest, and two nightstands.

A pastor and his wife lived downstairs. I was able to tell that the pastor and his wife did not like my mother from the moment we moved in. I quickly realized that their dislike for her meant they were not going to look out for me or help me if I had to run downstairs to escape the molestation. I was right. They were no help; they did not want to have anything to do with us!

There was a drug house two doors down from our house, and the guy who lived in the house was named Wade. I can never recall meeting Wade's mother. I knew he was in my age range, but I never knew much about his family. However, I do know he ran the house. I wanted to get close to Wade and his friend because I felt they would look out for me. Even though I wanted to get to know Wade and his family, I could never make myself walk over to their house. I was too shy and thanks to Al, I was afraid of getting raped.

I was already dealing with enough concerns. I was trapped and alone with no one to turn to for any help. I would pray and cry myself to sleep, but the pain was still there the next day.

There was one thing that made me feel better, and that was music. I always loved music. I used to listen to a song called *Safe in the Arms of God* by Janet Lynn Skinner. She is a gospel recording artist from Cleveland, Ohio. I was 15 years old when that song came out, and I fell in love with it.

The Lord he heard a cry,
for I was blind but now I see.

Now that I'm safe
in the arms of God,
nothing in this world can bother me.

Safe In The Arms of God
Janet Lynn Skinner

Chapter Three

After School

I attended Alexander Hamilton Jr. High in Cleveland, Ohio. I remember getting in trouble at school and my mother was notified of my behavior. When I arrived home from school, I was greeted by Al and my mom. I knew this wasn't going to be good.

Al told me to remove my clothes. My mom sat on the sofa, and I was sitting on the loveseat. I looked at my mom as I was taking off my clothes. I was amazed that she was going to allow me to take off my clothing in front of this man. He told me to take my panties and bra off also.

Al was a big man around 6 feet tall and about 300lbs. He took his belt off and whipped me. I don't know what hurt more, the whipping or watching my mother sit there and allow it to happen.

I looked over at my mom, and she had somewhat of a smile on her face. My feelings were hurt that she allowed this crazy man to beat me! Once the whipping ended, I was told to go take a bath. My skin was bleeding, and I was in pain.

The issues I dealt with weren't just inside my home, they seemed to follow me outside of my home as well...

While attending school at Alexander Hamilton, I had a gym teacher named Mr. Elder. He had concerns about why I never got dressed for gym class, so he gave me an F. I was unable to get dressed for gym class because I felt ashamed. I found it hard to change into shorts or even a swimsuit for swimming classes. The abuse from Al left me feeling very self-conscious about my body.

After failing his class the second time around, he yelled my name and said, "Frazier, to my office now."

Once I arrived at his office, he grabbed my breast and said, "If you allow me to do this to you, I will pass you in my class."

At that moment, I wanted to DIE! I was mad, and I felt like TRASH! I pushed a desk over, and I ran out of his office. It was the end of the school day. I told two of my friends what happened because I desperately needed to tell someone and I had no one else to share this with.

After sharing what had taken place in that office with Mr. Elder with one of my friends, she went home and told her mother what happened to me in school. I was not going to share the information with my mom because I was convinced that she would not care.

My friend, Tina, shared the information with her mother. Her mother called and told my mom what took place in the school that day. When Mother asked me what happened and I told her, she seemed to be calm and upset at the same time. I was confused by her reaction seeing that what Mr. Elder did was not that much different than what was happening inside our home. She never seem to care about that, so why was she being concerned about this?

Mother took me to school that next day and spoke with the staff about her concerns. She even spoke to several different people on the board of education!

I was informed by my mother that Cleveland board of education felt I was lying on Mr. Elder because he failed me. They wanted to remove me from the school and send me to Charles A. Mooney, a school on the westside of Cleveland. I was not upset that I was leaving

Alexander Hamilton. However, I was upset and confused on how she could allow them to remove me.

Nothing was done to Mr. Elder for his actions. I knew my mother to be a liar, so I was never certain if the story she told me was true. For all I know, she could have just removed me from the school herself. I cannot recall anyone speaking to me about my allegations or taking any statement from me. I had no reason to lie on Mr. Elder.

Later, as an adult, I ran into old friends, and the subject came up about what I went through in school. I told them about what my gym teacher had done to me.

One of the guys said, "Wait was the teacher name, Mr. Elder?"

I replied, "Yes, how do you know him?"

He said, "He was the gym teacher at Wilbur Wright Jr. High School."

I was amazed, and I said, "Really?"

He said, "Yes, he was removed from the school because he was touching on the girls in the locker room."

I couldn't believe what I was hearing. After all these years, there was finally something to corroborate my story.

"Would you share the story with my mom," I asked.

He said, "Sure, I will."

After he shared the story with my mother, she had a blank look on her face. She never once said I am sorry or anything.

This was just one of many times where my mother never came to my rescue. Now you see why I have always been certain that my mother never cared

about me!

Chapter Four

Al Goes to Prison for Other Crimes

Al had a long criminal record. Although he would go back and forth to jail, his time spent in prison was never long enough for me because I was happy when he was away. I would get upset when my mother would make me go to visit him in prison.

I remember those long rides from Cleveland, Ohio to Mansfield, Ohio, Lucasville, Ohio, Lima, Ohio and Columbus, Ohio. Those were the prisons where Al served time in jail. I was always sad knowing that I had to sit in front of the man who was violating me.

It didn't help that my mother was aware. He wanted me to hug him once we arrived and when we were leaving. He would rub my breast each time with my mom standing right beside me. She never said anything.

I can also remember him being placed in halfway homes once he was released. We would visit him there as well. Al's crimes were mainly drug and robbery related. He abused drugs badly. I remember seeing him use needles and taking different drugs. His addiction was so bad that he would even steal the rent money for drugs.

My mom worked as a nurse at Judson Manor for years. She made enough to support the household, but not enough to help a person on drugs.

Al would sell meat on the streets of Cleveland. Some days, he would even sell spoiled meat to get high off drugs. I was happy when he would go to prison, but it seemed he would never stay in jail long enough for me to recover. It appeared that prison would never change Al. He would say, "I am a changed person, and I

am going to do right this time around."
But he never did.

I used to say to myself, "I pray he
die in prison." I wanted Al dead because
then I would not have to deal with him
getting in my bed with me.

In 1984, I was 13-years-old, and
my cousin, Yvette, introduced me to a guy
named Troy Miller. Yvette was living on
Fuller off 93rd and Kinsman in Cleveland,
Ohio. Troy lived a few blocks away on
Harris Court. I was not allowed to talk to
boys on the phone at the time, but Yvette
was. She was allowed more freedom than

I was and could hang out and just be a kid.

Troy asked for my phone number, but I wouldn't give it to him. I knew my mother would never allow it. So, I would have him call my grandfather's house on weekends when I would stay at his home. During the week when I was at my mother's house, I would rush in from school and call him before she got home from work.

Troy was kind and sweet to me, but I was afraid to meet him in person. We were only talking over the phone at the time. We talked over the phone for two years before I would give in and meet face to face. I was scared because I lied about my age. He was five years older than myself. But I also didn't want to meet Troy in person because I hated my dark skin.

I started running away from home around age 15. The goal was to escape the pain and sleepless nights living in a home with two crazy people. I would run away to my boyfriend, Troy's house.

Troy was five years older than me. When I was 15, he was already 20-years-old. He didn't know my real age and I was ashamed for lying to him, but I was afraid that if he knew my real age, he wouldn't want to be with me and I'd lose the one person who was kind to me. I felt safe with Troy and couldn't risk losing him, which is what almost happened.

When I was 16, I became pregnant by Troy. My mom made me get an abortion, and she also tried to file rape charges against Troy because of my age. So, I had to confess the truth to her that I'd been lying and that Troy didn't know my real age.

I was upset that she would do this because I was dealing with molestation inside the home, and nothing was done to stop *that* abuse. Here she was again attempting to punish people outside our home over what was going on inside our home. It was very frustrating and confusing for me.

I also could not understand how my mom was active in the church, but was living a life full of secrets and lies. Turns out Al was married to someone else, but he lived with us!

Between 1985-1987, my mom legally changed her last name to her boyfriend Al's last name in order to make people think they were married. She didn't tell me, I learned the information on my own (in the 90's it was considered public information). I was amazed and embarrassed that she had changed her last name because I could not understand how she could live 'in sin' and still be an 'active saint' in the church. She was after all, living with another woman's husband!

I would get upset when she came to the school, and my teachers would address her as Ms. Frazier. She would correct them. She was such an embarrassment to me when I was in school.

Chapter Five

Living Life as an Only Child

I disliked being the only child. I felt life would have been better having a sister or a brother. My mother came from a large family. She is one of ten, with six brothers and three sisters. I am the oldest grandchild.

I always felt like my uncles and aunts should have protected me from the horrible things that were going on inside our home. But instead, they closed their eyes and acted like they did not know what was going on with me. They still have their eyes closed and claim they were not aware of what took place.

That was a lie!

As I got older, I would share information with various people in the Frazier family. No one offered to help me or even show me any kind of concern. My uncles and aunts never like Al, but at the same time they would laugh and spend time with him. I felt that was fake and that they should have been more concerned about my welfare rather than pleasing their sister.

My mother is the oldest child, and I think they might have feared her and how she would have reacted if they had gotten involved. Or maybe they were just *loyal* to her.

I guess I will never understand the term *ride or die* in relation to siblings seeing that I do not have any. People fail to realize that I had no one, but God. They felt everything was fine in our household regardless of what they knew at that time. As long as my mom, their sister, said that everything was ok, that was all that mattered to the family. Regardless of how close I tried to get to my uncles and aunts, they always seemed distant towards me.

Now that I'm older, they have shown their true colors by continuing to show me no concern or love. Knowing that I'm am the only child, I expected more from my family and wanted them to accept *me*.

Because of their unwillingness to get involved in my life when I was being abused, I find that I do not care about having a relationship with the family. I refuse to listen to the sad excuses of, "I did not know."

I have love for them because I know God requires me to do that, but I don't have to interact with them. The few family members with whom I do have a relationship, I thank God for, and I keep it moving. I see most of the Frazier family at funeral services, and that's enough for me.

I thank God for my grandfather. He always seemed to care about me and what was going with me. However, Mr. Frazier passed away in 2014. I do miss him.

In high school, I attended John Adams High in Cleveland, Ohio. I was kicked out because I hit a boy with a desk. He pulled my bra strap and ran off. I was already dealing with sexual abuse in my home, so I was unable to be friendly towards other people touching me in ways that I considered sexual. My mom came to the school, took me the juvenile detention center, and left me there. I was scared, but the officers told me that they could not lock me up. They were going to send me to a safe place. At that moment, I knew my mother was crazy, and I never wanted to see her again.

I reached out to my grandfather and told him what was going on. He showed up at the children's service building in Cleveland, Ohio and picked me up.

My grandfather was living in Riverside Park Apartments on Parkmount in Cleveland. It was also known as the "ROCK" near the Hopkins Airport. I was happy to be with my grandfather because I was out of the house with my crazy mom and her live-in boyfriend. My grandfather was good to me, and he allowed me to stay with him as long as I wanted to stay.

My mother came to visit my grandfather, her father, and she started an argument with me. My grandpa asked her to leave. I was happy to have someone stand up for me. I felt safe with my grandfather.

Although living with my grandfather was not the safest place for a child to be due to the company he kept and the lifestyle he allowed me to live (I had too much freedom and that wasn't necessarily a good thing for a young girl, but grandparents are usually more relaxed in the discipline area), I must say it was better living with him than with my mom.

My mother seemed to inflict pain on me at every turn. It hurt me that she loved a man more than she loved or cared about me. After being removed from John Adams, I dropped out of school in the 9th grade. She cared even less about my education and never pushed me to go back to school. After having my children, I set a goal to earn my high school diploma before my boys entered school. My mother told me that, "I should not even worry about getting a diploma."

WOW! I was shocked that a human being could say that to a person.

Even though I didn't have the support of my mother, I went back to school and earned my high school diploma, a career diploma (private investigator), an Associate's degree in Criminal Justice, a Bachelor's degree in Criminal Justice, and I am 6 classes away from my Master's degree in Criminal Justice. I thank God that I never allowed my mother's inability to support me to deter me from advancing.

My mother would often send me to Inkster Michigan in the summertime to visit with my grandmother (her mom), my aunts, and my uncles. She put me on the Greyhound bus, and I would be picked up once I arrived in Michigan. I got off the bus and went to the Burger King inside of the bus station.

Living life as an only child was hard. It was even harder living with a woman who didn't seem to see me or love me. I felt like a prisoner. The Frazier family reunions were held the first Saturday in

August. I would always have to help my mother with cooking while the other grandchildren were able to play and have fun with each other. I was a lost little girl who wanted to die.

I had a few cousins with whom I was close, but they were raised differently. They were allowed to do more than I could do. I had one cousin who I was always close with; her name was Kadotta Frazier (aka Dottie). Dottie is the one person in this family that has always shown support. When I got married in 1992, she was in my wedding she has never missed a moment in my life. She is the one cousin who attends graduations, birthday dinners, and even attends church with me sometimes. Dottie is the one person in the family that always believed me about how crazy her aunt (my mother) was.

As stupid as it may sound, I was glad to get away from the abuse in the home, but I would get homesick and miss my mother.

Chapter Six

Having My Children

I had my first child in 1991 and my second in 1992. I felt that I finally had people in my life who were going to love me for me; my husband and my children.

Wow was I wrong!

My kids have been brainwashed by my mother which is my fault. I should have removed her from their lives when they were little kids.

Being the only child, family was always important to me. I didn't want my boys to grow up isolated from their family so I chose not to remove her from their lives. I understood that these would be her *only* grandchildren because I was sure I was not going to have any more kids. I always wanted a little girl, and never wanted boys. Perhaps it was so I could nurture the little girl inside of me. But I guess that was not a part of God's plan for me.

I must admit my mother was a great help to us when the children were younger. I felt like I had twins seeing that they were only 14 months apart; it was hard some days to handle both of them while also trying to have a date night with my husband, but we managed to make it happen.

Mom Gets Sick

Between 1994-1995, my mother became ill, and I had to stop working as a nurse. She would later need help paying her rent until she was approved for her disability benefits. In the meantime, my mother had to move into the house with my husband, kids, and myself. No one else in the family would or could take her (Please keep in mind she is the oldest child of 10 children). Maybe they felt by her having an adult child, there was no need to worry because I would have it covered.

I was trying to be a good daughter and to help my mother as much as possible. In 1997, we bought our first house on 14005 Rexwood in Cleveland, Ohio. The home was large and roomy enough for my mom to have her own bedroom (Please keep in mind that we were in our early 20's buying a house with little to no understanding of what homeownership was or what to expect).

My mother was a great help with the kids, cooking, cleaning, and all that good stuff, but she tried to take over my family for some reason. I told her that Al was not allowed in my home or near my children. I did not trust him!

One day we left the children with my mom, and when we returned home, my oldest son informed us that Al had been at our house. I was upset and asked my mom why she would allow this man in my home against my wishes? I can't recall her reply, but it was not a good one!

After 2-3 years of my mother living with us in the new house, things were getting out of control, and I had to ask her to leave. She moved with a childhood friend in South Euclid which was about 20 minutes from my home. The childhood friend started to treat me strangely because I had put my mother out of my home (Please understand that I was always that child who made sure I looked out for my mom).

Living in a home with a mother who showed me no love was hard and painful at the same time. She always told me that I did not have anyone but her when I was a child. She told the truth and a lie at the same time. I did not have anyone, and I did not have her either. I love you, mother, for telling me that when I was younger!

Regardless of what people say about my parenting skills, I made sure that I was watchful over my sons and made certain no one was touching them in a sexual way. I also made sure that my sons walked out of my house with high school diplomas.

Wow, I wish my mother had cared that much about me

Chapter Seven

Love Hate Relationship

I want you all to understand that I loved my mom, but she never loved me! I respect her for raising me in the church, teaching me how to wear pantyhose, slips, etc. She made sure that I knew how to clean, wash clothes, and prepare meals.

I swear I was abused when it came to cleaning, but I can say I love her for teaching me basic life skills that I use each day. I thank God that I stayed away from the street life and maintained a foundation with God.

Mental illness is real! My mother had and currently has a mental illness that requires attention for which she refuses to seek help.

I used to sit in my room and talk to my teddy bear when I was younger. I would say, "I do not like my mother." I know that was mean to say, but I was a child. Today, I say, "I do not like my mother's ways."

I am hoping for a relationship with her, but I am doubtful that it will happen. I do wish her the best.

I am not going lie and tell you that I pray for her because I do not! I left her on the altar years ago. I prayed my prayer for her years ago.

I love my mom, but I don't understand why she did not protect me from people who abused me in a sexual way.

I realize now that Jesus loved me, and He gave me the strength to make it through the unbearable nights and days.

My mother's birthday is July 23 and I can recall never missing acknowledging that day. When I was around 12 years old, I asked some of her friends if I could do some housework for them to earn money to give her a party for her birthday.

Of course, no one allowed me to do any work; they all gave me money to buy the food for the party. At that time, my mom was working 3pm-11pm. I walked from East 139th Street to 144th. There was a grocery store at 14301 Kinsman Road back in the 80's. After I bought all of the food and ordered the cake, I had money left over that I tried to give back to the people who gave me money. No one wanted the money back, so I took the left over money and bought a gift and decorations.

I had enough time to get home, to cook, and to decorate the house. The guests started to arrive around 10:00 pm. Once my mother arrived, we turned off the lights and yelled, "Surprise" when she entered the room. It was one of our happier memories.

Mother's Day came around that following year, and mom gave me money to buy school shoes at Randall Mall in Warrensville Heights, Ohio 44128.

I was allowed to ride the bus with a friend to buy school shoes and lunch. I knew Mother's Day was coming, and I wanted to buy her something nice.

Instead of buying shoes and lunch, I went shopping for her at May Company. I even had the gifts wrapped in the store.

When I arrived home with gifts and no shoes, she whipped me with no clothes on. I was sad and hurt. I knew she never loved me, but to get beat was painful. I understood that she gave me money to buy shoes, and I should have followed her orders and I didn't.

I realized that I had a good heart at an early age, and I have always been a giver, not a taker. Once I became an adult, I would still buy presents for my mom for Christmas, for her birthday, for

Mother's Day, and for Valentine's Day. I even gave her a big birthday dinner at the Marriott Hotel in 2007.

One thing I can say my mother did was to make sure I had the best of everything – on the outside. No one could tell that I was being abused in the home. I was spoiled in that regard.

Mother also made sure that I was not exposed to some of the bad things teenagers were into. When I look around at my peers, I thank God I was raised in the church and have no regrets of not being allowed to party, drink, or hang out with the wrong group of people.

But there were a lot of things that she got wrong. I was not allowed to do things that kids my age should have been allowed to do like going to high school games and different social activities. Instead I was at home cooking full course meals and doing adult house chores.

I missed my childhood and was forced to become an adult much sooner than I should have. I dislike that I had to grow up quickly and become an adult sooner than my peers. Molestation is something no one in the world should have to deal with.

I often wonder how my family feels knowing they covered for their sister and allowed me to deal with years of sexual abuse?

This is why I've dedicated my life to the advocay of children. I refuse to know that a child is being abused and not speak up. It seems common these days for kids to deal with sexual assault. People close their eyes like they do not see the signs.

In addition to speaking out about my abuse, I had to also acknowledge the fact that nothing I do will change the past or even make my mother love me or care about the hurt she caused and allowed in my life. I now have to love and care for me. I now have to protect myself and through my story, help others who have experienced what I have overcome.

Chapter Eight

Thank God, for Troy

Mother put me out when she found out I was pregnant at the age of 16. Hearing the words, "Get out my house" were hurtful words to hear from a mother who knew I had nowhere to go at 11:00 pm. At that time, we were living on 123rd Signet. I would have to walk to Kinsman Road to get on the number 14 bus which would take me to 93rd Kinsman Road. I was headed to the one person I knew would be there for me, Troy.

Troy lived on Harris Court which is one block from 93rd Kinsman. Troy would meet me at the bus stop to make sure I was safe after being put out of the house. Troy has always been there for me.

That's why I was so confused when my mother threatened to press charges against him when I became pregnant by Troy at the age of 16.

I was underage, but Troy didn't know that. I had also been underage when my mother allowed Al to abuse me too, yet she had not attempted to stop it or even report it.

Once again, I stress that mental illness is a serious sickness. I admitted that I had been lying about my age, and Troy was not aware that I was underage. Troy was the only real person in my life at that time, and I knew he cared about me and tried to keep me from all harm. I just couldn't understand how she was adamant about protecting me from some people, but not all people.

I know you are wondering, "What happened to the baby?" Well my mother went to my uncles and informed them that I was pregnant and the next thing I knew, I was having an abortion.

One of my uncles was going to have me come to his state to have the abortion done. I can't recall what happened with that plan of action. I was hurt. I did not want to have the abortion. I felt the baby would help me overcome my pain.

Maybe a month later, in July of 1989, I found myself at the Preterm Abortion Clinic. I was sick, mad, and I wanted to die! Troy was not allowed to be around me because my mother had made his life hell. She was saying she would have him locked up.

At that point, I felt it would be better for him and for us if I honored her request until I reached the legal age for Troy and I to date. We were never totally apart though. He would make sure to call me each year on my birthday!

About a year after Troy and I stopped seeing each other, I started dating and ended up getting married to someone else 2 or 3 years later. In 1991, I had my first child and the second son came in 1992. The brainwashing from my mother has caused the boys to have different feelings towards me. We don't have a relationship. I am okay with the way things are because I gave them the best I had and made sure no one was doing them wrong. I pray that God saves their souls and allows them to be successful men. That marriage lasted until 2005.

I ran back into Troy in 2006 and we started talking and sharing information with each other about where we were in life and our goals. I had no idea that we would get back together and eventually marry in 2008.

People around always knew about Troy because I always shared the story of how he looked out for me when I was younger. Troy did what he could do to help me. For that, I will always have respect for him and he will always be in my heart. I have to give credit, where it is due.

Troy has been my ongoing support over the many years of our marriage. What we have is like a pair of scissors, we cut anything that comes between us and that includes children, family members, and friends.

I can say Troy is my best friend, and I like the cool calm person he is. He allows nothing to worry him and always says, "It's going to be okay."

I thank God for giving Troy the strength to deal with the changes that took place in our life concerning the children and the ongoing fights with my mother. Troy never once told me not to deal with my mom, but he was not willing to keep dealing with the disrespect coming from her.

One day after telling Troy that I had a lot of faith in my uncles (my mother's brothers), Troy looked at me and said, "They were not good uncles because they did not protect you."

After he had made that statement, I thought about it and my reply was, "You are correct. Even if they wanted to stick by that fake story of not knowing what happened back then, they sure know now and they are still crazy and refuse to show me any love."

"It's a shame," Troy shook his head. "There are so many people in your family and they all sit around and pretend like they do not recall anything!"

Troy wears many hats in this marriage; some days he is my dad, my brother, or my uncle. I am sure he has learned that being married to an only child who has been through what I've been through requires him to play different roles.

I didn't need to think about it long. I knew that he was correct. Regardless of what you may think or how you feel, you should always be willing to help a child when you hear they are dealing with abuse.

With age and wisdom, I have learned I can't change my family or what happened in my past. Therefore, I have changed my way of thinking. To be honest, if I could hate them and still make it to Heaven, I would. I know I have to love them, but I am not required to deal with them.

My advice is once you learn that people do not care about you, get away from that negative energy.

BLOOD IS NOT THICKER THAN WATER IN MY CASE, BUT THE BOND I HAVE WITH JESUS REPLACES SOME OF THE HURT! I am bruised, but I am not broken!

Chapter Nine

Church Life

Growing up in the church was good *and* bad for me. We switched churches when I around 13-years-old to Pure Love COGIC in Cleveland Ohio. I did not like this church because the pastor would pick on me and say strange things. I mentioned it to my mother, and I told her I did not like when he said things like, "You are pretty," and "If I was not married and you were older, you would be my wife."

Those were things he would say in front of the church. I was confused that all these adults could think it was okay for the pastor to say this to a child.

I am happy that I didn't allow that experience to deter me from going to church anymore. I still attend church (JUST NOT THAT CHURCH ANYMORE).

Often, people allow the bad things that happen to them in church to keep them away from **all** churches. I refuse to stay away from God's house. He has been too good to me through the years. However, I make sure that I pay close attention to the way pastors (or people period) interact with children.

The pattern of abuse begins to get real clear when you experience it over and over. Once again, no one saw anything wrong with this man saying these crazy things to me.

I remember spending the night with his daughter. I was around 14-years-old. The daughter and I shared a full-sized bed. Her older brother came downstairs in the room and tried to put his penis in my butt.

I started moving around to wake his sister up, and he left the room. I was scared and confused, and I asked God, "Why me?"

This same son is a pastor now, here in Cleveland, Ohio. I pray that he did not inherit his father's abusive mentality.

When I told my mother what happened to me at their home, she overlooked the whole story and kept moving on with her life.

Parents, aunts, uncles, sisters, brothers, and people, please listen to children when they say someone is saying inappropriate things or touching them in inappropriate places.

Chapter Ten

I Am Different for Many Reasons

I know that God made me the way He wanted me to be. I have always asked God why He allowed me to go through what I had to deal with. I still did not have the answers to my questions, but I can say that I am a stronger person in spite of what happened to me.

I refuse to allow people to tell me I am weak because I keep talking about the abuse I dealt with. NO, I AM STRONG

BECAUSE I AM BRINGING AWARENESS TO THE WORLD!

I do tend to have trust concerns when it comes to dealing with people. I feel I am concerned because my mother failed to protect me from harm as a child, so maybe I over compensate but I feel it's better to be safe than sorry.

I have learned some things about myself when it comes to trusting others. People will try to hurt you for no reason at all. My mother is a great example of that.

She had no reason to allow Al to abuse me. She also had no reason to allow any of the other people who abused me to do so. If you can't trust your parents as a child, who can you trust? I know now that I can place all trust in God for He cares for me, and He loves me.

I have not talked to or seen my mother in 3 or 4 years, and I must say these have been the best years of my life. I can't allow myself to go back to abusive relationships. I love her, and I forgive her, but I have peace. I wish her the best in life. I pray that God allows her to see that her little girl suffered a long time from her not protecting her from hurt, harm, and danger.

My goal is to help others overcome sexual abuse with the support of God. I have always had the heart to help others even when I know they don't want the help at that time.

I have always wanted a shoulder to cry on and wanted that shoulder to be my mother, but she didn't give it to me. I understand that God wanted my attention and wanted me to lean on Him. Thankfully, I did.

I have good days, and yes, I still have bad days too. The scars are still there, and keep me aware of who I am and where I have been. I do not know what God has planned for the future, but I know I will allow Him to order my steps.

I have been planning and talking about writing this book for 20 years, but I allowed fear to overtake my mind. I was concerned about people and how they would feel. I can't worry about people's feelings any longer. My job is to help bruised, hurt, and depressed people overcome the past and follow their dreams no matter how bad life has been. I want them to know that although they have been bruised, they don't have to live a life that is broken.

I currently have a nonprofit organization called *Follow Your Dreams Academy*. Helping people pursue their dreams is something that I have a passion for. My goal is to assist individuals who have dropped out of high school, earn their high school education. I also help those who have dealt with any abuse to get the services that they need to live a healthy life and be the best they can be to themselves and others.

I am an ordinary person who was dealt an extraordinary hand, but I refuse to play the blame game and use my past as an excuse not to do better. I could say, "It is my mother fault that I dropped out of school, have low self-esteem, and dislike being around people, etc.," but why would I do that? My mom is living her life, and I have to do the same for myself. I will always have an open door to help people who want to help themselves. I cried for help from family members as a child, and they overlooked me. I will never neglect a child's cry for help!

God is not pleased with anyone who ignores children.

My Memories

Photo Gallery

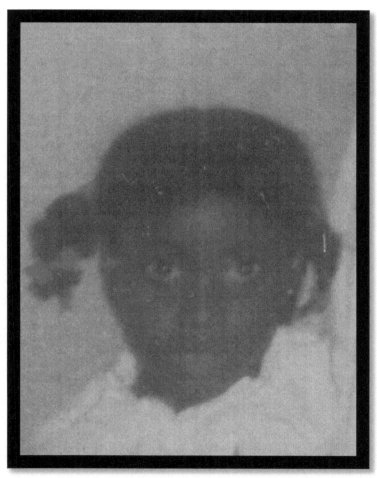

Photo 1 Childhood Photo (age 6-8)

Photo 2Childhood Photo (age 8)

Photo 3 Young Adulthood (age 21)

Photo 4 Author and favorite cousin

Photo 5 Childhood Home (East side Cleveland OH)

Photo 7 Grandfather's Home (Cleveland Ohio)

Photo 6 Grandfather's Home (Cleveland, Ohio)

Photo 8 Criminal Justice Degree

Photo 9 Criminal Justice Degree (With Troy)

Photo 10 Troy and Sherena

Photo 11 2016 Labor Day Parade

Photo 12 University of Phoenix Associate's degree

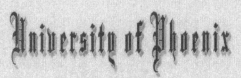

University of Phoenix

Upon the recommendation of the Faculty,
University of Phoenix does hereby confer upon

Sherena Frazier Miller

the degree of

Bachelor of Science in Criminal Justice Administration

with all the rights, honors and privileges thereunto appertaining.

In witness whereof, the seal of the University and the signature as authorized
by the Board of Trustees, University of Phoenix, are hereunto affixed,
this thirtieth day of June, in the year two thousand sixteen.

Chairman, Board of Trustees

President

Photo 13 University of Phoenix Bachelor degree's

Photo 14 Author on wedding day

Book Club Discussions

Why do you think Sherena's mother did nothing to protect or support her daughter?

What role do you think Sherena's appearance played in other's noticing that she was being abused?

Can you look at a person and tell they are being abused?

Have you ever loved someone you knew hurt you or who was supposed to protect you and didn't?

Why do you think there were so many abusers in Sherena's life?

Based on clues in the story, how do you think Sherena's past impacts her current life?

A Place for Your Bruises

Sherena Frazier-Miller

A Journal

Writing truly is therapeutic. Often, it can help bring clarity to a situation. Once you can see yourself and your circumstances in a truthful manner, you can begin the process of healing.

Writing affords you the ability to recognize patterns that you may not be able to recognize otherwise. I encourage you to use the following pages to begin releasing some of the toxic things in your life.

Praying for your healing,

~Sherena Frazier-Miller

A Journal

A Journal

A Journal

A Journal

A Journal

A Journal

A Journal

A Journal

A Journal

A Journal

A Journal

A Journal

A Journal

A Journal

A Journal

A Journal

About the Author

One critical thing I have learned in my life is that I deserve respect from everyone whom has contact with me. If respect cannot be given freely, that person does not belong in my life.

I share my story in hopes of helping others overcome the sexual abuse in their lives. Such experiences remain in our lives all of our lives. It is not something that one day I will get over it. This is just not true. It does not happen in such a way. Sharing my story of childhood molestation as a motivational speaker can encourage others to seek help and to report molestations especially of children. No child should have a story like mine. Some people like me can and will help.

Lastly, I use my life story to illustrate that anyone can overcome any challenging situation with the proper help. I hope to inspire others. You can make it and be successful in life. Follow your dreams! Never give up! I am following my dreams. I know God has been with me on this long walk of life.

Contact Sherena Frazier-Miller

Website:

Sfraziermiller.com

Facebook:

@Sherena Frazier-Miller

Instagram:

@sfraziermiller

Eiffel Tower Books

an imprint of

The Butterfly Typeface Publishing.

Your Story. Your Life. Your Words.

Contact us for all your

publishing & writing needs!

Iris M Williams

PO Box 56193

Little Rock AR 72215

(501) 823 - 0574

www.butterflytypeface.com

Made in the USA
Columbia, SC
11 December 2020